We A

A Child's Journey to Womanhood

Crystal Rose

WE ARE ROYALTY
Copyright © 2020 by Crystal Rose Patterson

All rights reserved. Neither this publication nor any part of this publication may be reproduced or transmitted in any form or by any means, electronic or mechanical, including photocopying, recording or any information storage and retrieval system, without permission in writing from the author.

poetrybycrystalrose.blogspot.com
crystalrose543@gmail.com

Cover, text design and layout by Beth Crane, WeMakeBooks.ca
Edited by Andrea Lemieux
Author photograph by Danielle Byles

Print ISBN: 978-1-4866-2247-4
eBook ISBN: 978-1-4866-2248-1

Word Alive Press
119 De Baets Street, Winnipeg, MB R2J 3R9
www.wordalivepress.ca

Cataloguing in Publication may be obtained through Library and Archives Canada

I thank my Lord and Saviour Jesus Christ for dying on the cross and saving me. I love him so much. I want to thank my dearly beloved and beautiful mother Sharon Patterson, for supporting and encouraging me throughout my career. She helped me to pursue my dream. She has been a blessing.

Contents

Child Abuse 1
Bath Experience: Gritty Vomit 2
Child Abuse Continues 3
That Nighttime
   Runaway Child 4
Mom Came Home 6
Mom Is Here 7
Back Home at Mom's 8
Broken Heart 9
Church, 1995 10
Mom, Are You There? 11
Child's Inquiry of God 12
Encouraged 14
The Definition of a Girl's
   Dream Encounter 15
Uncle 17
The Effects of My Abuser:
   Desperate to Know Christ 18
Looking for Love 19
Fearfully and Beautifully Made
   Girl 20
Friends Are Like Rocks 21
I Confess to My Mom 22
My Mom Has Been through
   Trials and Pain 23
Forgiveness 25
Forgiveness during
   Dinnertime 26
Rejection during
   University 28
Story of Love:
   Luke 7:37-47 32
Healing for Porcelain Dolls .. 34
Little Princess 35
Ashes Traded for Beauty 37
A Bride
   (in the Eyes of Christ) 38
His Heartbeat Yearns
   for Her 39
The Fragrance of a Beautiful
   Soul (Learning to Love
   Myself) 41

Elegant and Beautiful 42	Blood-Royal of Heaven 74
Chocolate Queen 44	We Are Royalty in His Eyes . 75
Ballerina-Dress Daughter 45	No More 77
Treasure in My Father's Eyes 46	I Don't Need to Search Any Longer 78
I'm a Beautiful Red Rose 48	Confidence 79
Rhyming One Beautiful Queen 49	Her Worth Redeemed 80
	Her Seditions 81
"Face Like the Sun": Qualities of Mine 50	Christ's Asian Princess 83
Freedom 52	Beautiful Mannequin in a Glass to Him 84
Liberty in Jesus 54	Royal Highness 85
Hopeful 56	Black and Beautiful 86
It Bothers You 58	Afrocentric Beauty 87
Jealousy Kills 59	Marvellous Afro 88
I Am Sacred 61	He Got Married to Me on the Cross 89
Rejection 62	
Memories of My Father 67	Continue to Rise 90
Restored Lily 69	River of Rain 91
I Feel Fat 71	Discrimination during University Years 92
The Media Told Me Who I Am 72	Racial Borders 93
Valuable 73	Beautiful Gaze 95

Accept Christ and He Will
  Give You Eternal Life 97
My Story 98
What Does It Mean? 99
The Essence of Life
  (Personal Testimony) 100
You Are a Champ 102
Ex-Boyfriend: Courtship ... 103
Why He Loves Me 105
Beautiful 106
I Exhaled the Remains 109
Part Two 111
First Love 113
Forgiveness 118

Child Abuse

In summer 1990, Brampton.
Six years old, looking at
scraggly trees from a
two-story
town-home.
Cousins and I stay
with Auntie for
two weeks,
until Mom could get
on her feet.
Auntie's psychosis.
She was raped when she
was young. As I got older,
I hated her.

My mom's sister
was accused of child abuse
of many sorts.
When she was in a rage,
she took her anger out
on anyone in her way,
like a storm ripping
the leaves.
She once spun her
daughter by the
hair, as if she were
a helicopter.
She often left scars
on tiny hearts.

BATH EXPERIENCE: GRITTY VOMIT

In that same summer of
1990, the very first week
my cousins and I
were pretending
to be Cinderella,
except my mahogany face,
was now a pale-light colour.
Auntie put an unknown
ingredient in my tea that
made my stomach churn.
Along with my two
cousins, we ran
past her embroidered
carpet, careful not to spill,
purple lipped.
My body now
bent over the bathtub
to get rid of it.
Celena curled over
the lip of the
sink doing the same.

Auntie's body
now looming over mine,
watching, as three
little princesses are
spewing red gritty vomit,
only to upset her
for vomiting the nice
tea she had made.
She coerced us
into eating, until her
bathtub was shiny again.

Child Abuse Continues

Our second week.
Waking up to bacon
and eggs.
I hope she doesn't
do anything else.
I saw her face, and
my body quivered.
We played
all day and begged her
to let us go outside.
More happened
at the house,
and memories could take
me back.
She threw hot
water on Tatiana's back.
My memories of us.
We should be
valued and cherished.

It was nighttime, and
sizzling water was boiling
in a kettle with the heat
at maximum so she
could drown Tatiana
with it in her sleep.
I witnessed
the way my cousin's
body clattered from the
boiling hot water just off
the high-heat burner.
I would have faced her
but I was too scared,
so I hid.

That Nighttime Runaway Child

Sunset is beaming.
Dear reader, on that same
   night when she threw
   hot water, we slept like
   mannequins in our bed.
We were hoping to keep her
sane.
The next morning the
   sunrise is glowing
and the kids are playing
   hopscotch.
We agree to run away
from her rules that restrict
us from playing outside.
We huddle like football
players, plotting our next
scheme.
The bed is still
soaked from my cousin's
accident.
We manage to escape,
and retreat to a playground
nearby.
Outside from dawn 'til
dusk the swings
rock back and forth.
Later kids begin to slowly
   leave to
be in their loving homes.
A few police patrol the
   playground, and
ask us who we are.
They have papers with
names that match the
names we confess.
We tell them we don't want
to go back, and confess of
   her torture.
The sounds of
children's voices aren't there.
Birds have deserted.

When we reach her door,
she lies, and says that we are
    liars.
I don't
recall if I was beaten,
but I remember we
scattered like roaches away
    from her blows, as she
    waved a broken
broom, trying to hit Tatiana
    on the back.
Angels consoling her.
I envisioned their big
    beautiful
wings clasping her body
    close.
Consoling every tear, the
abuser doesn't know better,
but I will protect your heart
through the beautiful young
ceramic Angels.

Mom Came Home

Two weeks had passed.
We barely make a sound.
As statues, we stand there,
tip-toeing back and forth.
Her laughter is hefty,
and her finger tips are blackened
from holding cigarette butts.
I have never seen anything as evil as this.
My head pressed the windowpane,
hoping to see her beautiful face.

Mom Is Here

Her face looked renewed,
elegant, the way she
wears her wrap skirt.
Her cheeks
glimmering from the joy.

She leaves her bags
parked on the floor
beside a nearby brown
couch.
To be held by her.
I buried my face
in her chest, to hide
the tears.

Back Home at Mom's

The second week of 1990.
From Auntie's house
we drove home.
Mom's face was a bit sad.
She had to leave us because
she had baby blues right after
she had me.
Her aunt was her
best friend, and the only one
at the time who was willing
to take care of me in Mom's
absence.

Looking for love,
I ran to receive his warm
    embrace.
His breath was fresh,
but I just wanted to feel
his chiseled face
against
my beautiful skin,
healing.

Broken Heart

My hands lift up,
and my face protrudes,
hoping that she will
find the tear stains
that were left behind.
Unable to express,
and ask, "Where have you been?"
Upset at the way Auntie
treated me. Finding my
voice, it's fluttering inside.

Church, 1995

Mom took us to church.
I loved wearing my fluttery
dress, so that I could feel like
   a princess.
The laughter of little
   children,
and the brown church, and a
Leader teaching me who
   Jesus was.
I remember reading a
   children's
Bible about this man named
   Jesus
who loved little children, and
   I remember
singing those songs.

It protected my heart
and planted a seed of Love.
I didn't know him,
I just knew that I felt loved,
and I never wanted to
be out of this sweet
   presence,
of this love, in the company
   of someone who made
   me feel safe;
as if I could feel no harm
   again.

Mom, Are You There?

I felt despondent.
I longed to express myself,
and as a baby dove
longs to fly, to
break past nest-life,
was beautiful,
but I couldn't express
my hurts.
I painted for days,
and I wrote for hours.
I loved fashion
because it was beautiful,
but every time I saw Mom,
my tears, and my voice,
   longed
to express themselves,
but they didn't know how.
So being alone,
was as where I sought this
   presence.
Further.

I cried out to this unknown
God, and I often prayed
that he would fill
the empty part.
I flew in class,
I painted very well,
but my voice was captured,
and locked.
I was quiet
and didn't raise my voice
when men took advantage.
I was an easy target,
and I didn't know that I
could say no.
A mother's love is what I
   cried for,
and even though I never
   received
love, I was able to give it
with the love of this
   presence.

Child's Inquiry of God

She missed my dad.
I've seen my mom, and how
  she loved her sisters,
and there was always chatter
about the way they treated
her, as a scapegoat.
I loved my mom's strength,
she was courageous.
She mentioned a beautiful
man named Christ, whom
  she encountered
when she was going through
  a depression.
Us, walking in the night,
  hearing Mom's
heart, I looked up at the sky.
I never feared looking up so
  high,
and for the first time
adulthood wasn't that scary.
The clouds were beautiful,
and the clouds looked like
snow, painted by a painter.
I felt a presence consuming
  my
mind, and asked my mom if
God was real.
Needing someone to talk to,
I often looked up to the sky.
Willow, wondering, where
God is and why.
One day walking,
face looking up at the
  beautiful sky,
asking Mom questions,
I, the same, and even
as a child I had to conjure
  enough
strength to love her.
A child doesn't know
that day I never told a soul.

I kept in order,
out of fear, I didn't
want to disrupt the green
    giant.

Encouraged

>Mom always spoke of Christ's love.
>Daddy placed a flower in my hair.
>I ran to receive his warm embrace.
>His breath was fresh,
>but I just wanted to feel
>his chiseled face against
>my beautiful skin,
>healing.

The Definition of a Girl's Dream Encounter

My mom has gone to
 Jamaica, 1995.
I am left with a friend of
 hers,
down the street.
She left her brother in
charge of her home.
A preteen,
learning to be
ladylike.
Baggy clothes
clung to my slim body.
It was summer outside.
I proceeded to go
back home for seconds.
To get a break
from being a pest at my
 mom's friend's.
My uncle was there.
He had just finished
smoking at the back door.
All too familiar,
pictionaries of the
little girl sitting
on Christ's lap,
except he gave
me a sinister eye.
I tried to envision
the little girl sitting on
Christ's lap,
desperately looking
out for a hug
when he extended
his arms.
Protection, and care,
under my mom's roof
was the same as whimsical
men misled
by lust.

Witnessing a whimsical
man mislead
by lust,
he saw a woman
instead of a daughter
mannequin, still,
I froze
as he frolicked
his hand lightly
down my yellow-black
wool shirt
and lay his fingers,
on my thin shirt,
on my chest.
There was silence!

I felt ceramic Angels
   watching,
and protecting me,
holding me close
inside their wings
to make sure that he
didn't probe further.

Beautiful Angels, letting
me know, and unveiling
the protecting hands of
Jesus.

Uncle

He stayed at Mom's house
for another week,
so I decided to remain
at my mom's friend's,
until Mom came back
home from Jamaica
when I could feel safe.

THE EFFECTS OF MY ABUSER: DESPERATE TO KNOW CHRIST

And I should be in love with him,
that is what the love of
Christ taught.
I wanted this God,
so I began a long journey
of wrestling thoughts of
suicide.

I was desperate
the love of Christ
is what I yearned
for because if anyone needed it,
I needed Him right now!

Looking for Love

The cool of the day feels
 sweet.
I outstretch my arms, as stars
 paint
the sky.
My breath heavy from rum.
Ready to fall in love with
Jesus again.
Screaming
at the top of my lungs,
asking Him to
restore intimate
parts of me, unfolding
my heart like leaflets,
and allowing Him
to heal my pain.

I open my heart up to God
 so that
he could soften the arduous
 heart,
tears flowing, being
released from their secret
 place
of long suppressed
emotions!

Fearfully and Beautifully Made Girl

It's now 2010.
I opened up Psalms 139:13-14.
The sun is shining
for you created my innermost being.
You knit me together in my
mother's womb.
I praise you because
I am fearfully and
wonderfully made.

Friends Are Like Rocks

The next day,
I place a flower in my hair.
Tea with a girlfriend,
to share the love of Jesus.

1 Confess to My Mom

Overcome abuse with love.
My bangles cling loosely
to my elongated arms,
and my eyes
are in love.
In the mirror,
for the first time,
my worth isn't defined
by the abuse of my uncle
and my aunt.
Despite it all I became a
   confident woman.

My Mom Has Been through Trials and Pain

My mom has been through
    trials and pain.
Rivals and shame.
Afraid to have a child in a
    world full of pain,
but she took a risk and had a
    beautiful daughter.
Promised that if she planted
    a seed she would give her
    water.
Hurt from the thoughts
    of raising me without a
    father,
but my smile and soothing
    presence reminded her of
    the radiance of a pearl.
A newborn untainted from
    the pollution of the
    world.

I was her gem, her Crystal,
    her precious baby girl.
So she decided to give me a
    valuable name.
A name with meaning and
    taste.
A name with feeling and
    praise.
A name with healing and
    grace.
She wanted to give me a
    name of dignity
because faith was all that
    she could give to me,
because she lived a life full
    of misery,
afraid that I should repeat
    her history.
To her, I am majestic,
like a crystal glass without
    blemish.

So valuable, royal, soothing,
and majestic.
In her eyes, I'm a crystal
glass so pure and
beautiful.
Without stain, or spot, so
she named me Crystal.

Forgiveness

It is 2010, and there are
many rumours that my
aunt will fly down.
She has been released from prison
for child-abuse allegations.

Forgiveness during Dinnertime

Chatter of family members.
Rumours that Auntie will
Come down to visit us again.
This time, I am twenty-six.

I don't know how,
but I obtain strength
to forgive her.
It is family time,
and I am reminded of
the scripture of love.
She walks into the room,
and her shame consumes
   her.
I give her my honour,
attention, and support.
The child is gone,
and I let love fill my
eyes, and tell her I love her.
I am happy to see her again.

My uncle stood
in the living room,
khaki pants,
dread hat,
bushy beard. by
the sliding door.
Summertime.
I gave my uncle
a big hug and told
him that I loved him too.

Young gazelle,
find the strength to forgive.
Mahogany-faced,
Doe-like
black and Asian
strong women.
We all go through it.
Somewhere along
life's journey,
our petals have been ripped

off by the aggression
of someone's hands,
by someone's verbal
abuse, but in the love of
Christ there is much
healing and forgiveness.

Love, Crystal.

Rejection during University

I yearn for whets beyond these walls, these corridors, so I crawl, open doors, whets beyond this wind, so I crave it like an addict. For your information my kind got talents, we rap and sing ballads, aspirations, and gifts, and we are more than just rum and splits. Because they don't cater to us—here they believe that if they give us a mantle we'll fail, they believe that all we'll amount to is drugs and jail; but black people are more than just cold and frail, but our skin colour is the colour of sun, but let me tell you what I mean when I thought I unlocked the door to his heart with my radiant smiles as he looked outside the wind embraced his limbs as the sun pierced my eyes, usually the wind would collide brush my black face, lift my moods, taste my kinky hair, intrude my space, but this time butterflies inside did paint my clouds with rainy days, so as I witnessed signs of his rainy-day tension within his cloud, it disrupted my soul seeing his angled eyebrows interrupt my soul, you're too black. So my heart departed from the sun made me know what was going on, rejection I could tell because his thoughts were interrupted

by ringing bells of their
word—rejection. I thought
I had unlocked his heart
with my soul, Ashanti black
beauty, but I was left with
miseries, rejection. Because
he was closed in, tampered,
saturated with trickery, I
wanted the rays of my smile
to emblazon his sadness,
dip him in a pool of moral
gladness, but rejection—
these words that he exhaled
fractured my mind, leaked
inside my soul, affected
my incite of black beauty,
because his words were
intrusive, elusive, my black
beauty blurred with words of
rejection that left my mind
in confusion. I wanted to
replace his ignorance with
my black beauty "intrude
him"—beauty like soot that
rises to the air, engraves
his heart with my spell and
takes him there to my black
beauty because I wanted
to tattoo his lips with my
black kiss, but his thoughts
were manipulated by ringing
bells of their—rejection. I
thought I unlocked the door
to his heart with my black
smiles, but he wouldn't let
me divorce his mind from
thoughts of these racist and
perilous times, so rejected,
we were just friends back
then, thought that we could
be more than but he wanted
to keep our distance, like
memories of my playpens,
so rejected, because my
skin tone kept us from
being more than mates,
so rejected that left me
feeling more than hate and

disconnected, so he divorced me, rejected so I felt rejected when I walked out of my house, thinking maybe if I permed my hair he would accept me as a spouse, but I grew up as a black queen, kinky-hair rats and mouse, but to choose you should I reject, Jamaican dialect, you done know at your European expense, so as I thought should I leave, or to European ideals be attached so our skins clashed like a boxing match rejection? This is what made me feel like I had to divorce myself from this bloody picture-rejection, because you abandoned me when you abandoned the other side of your mixture, so your pleas of I'm a mixed breed, my mother's white, and I have a dark skin-toned dad, but you guys, he rejected me because he said that my skin colour is too black, but you see when he rejected me, he neglected everything he had—Ashanti black beauty because every time I seen her, and you felt like her, and my pigment battled in the room. Then you had to choose like you were confused about your African roots. Face it, you neglected our skin tones like darkskinned girls pushed to the backside of music videos, like never really seeing black girls in herbal-essence commercials. Like never really seeing coloured cartoons and band aids the colour of maroons, so rejection, you made me feel

this way like our colour
was a disgrace, rejection, I
divorced myself from these
lies that society replays in
our minds that our skin
colour is like lice because
my colour is like the sun's
lights, black queens, not
stereotyped black fiends,
but black queens with the
expressions of queenly
persona, you guys we are
black queens.

"Face like the Sun." His face
looked something like the
moon's, reflecting, sparkling,
every time he smiled. His hair
sparkled, and was like coils,
silky, but thick curls.

Story of Love: Luke 7:37-47

Sin heavy from fornication,
sleeping around,
but when she heard
that Jesus was in town,
she submitted her will
to His leadership.

She knelt down before him
and wiped His feet
with her hair.
She poured from an
alabaster box
the richest of affairs.
Her expensive perfume
poured out.
She mixed it with tears.
She loved Jesus
passionately.
This is the story of love.

He fell in love
with her heart
as His eyes gleamed
like studs.
She poured out
her heart,
and He said to one of
His disciples, "Seest thou
this woman?...
I say unto thee,
Her sins, which are many
are forgiven,
for she loved much,"
and I finally get it!
Relationships are about
   loving
one another.

For years
I have wrestled
with the ability to
love because
of what they did,
but if Christ died for
me and forgave me,
then I need to forgive.

Healing for Porcelain Dolls

He thinks you're a beautiful
   girl.
I talk to a girlfriend of mine,
and she is caught up
in men.
My heart cries because
she is really a beautiful stem.
Her petals let out for any
man to come,
and the ringlets
in her eyes,
like the blackening
of the sun.
He thinks you're a beautiful
   girl.
I talk to a girlfriend of mine,
but she is a scared
bird rarely taking to the sky.

She wants to be
loved, eye shadow
on her eyes,
but I share my story
and tell her that she
is more beautiful inside.

Little Princess

There is healing, little girl,
teenager, young adult,
woman,
princess.
The one who traces
and smudges lipstick
all over her face,
to be noticed,
to be held in.
There is healing, little girl,
The one who twirls
her skirt in the sky,
the one who wishes
to be noticed by just
one's eyes.
Well, you should know
Something, little girl.
Christ thinks you're
　beautiful,
His jewel, his bride.

Memories used to paint the
　indoors of my mind,
and I played the defence,
as if I were slapping
　volleyballs away
from my direction.
I confessed, every
emotion,
of what my uncle did,
and for the first time
I felt free,
but leaving a sky,
leaving my perception clear
as day,
leaving my
tears to fall in God's bottle.

Disdained, trapped.
I tell someone for the first
　time.

I didn't realize that
I was a beautiful rose;
so long,
mildew on my mind.
His long fingers
traced my yellow-and-black
   patterned shirt,
and he left his
hand there,
resting
on my chest,
uninvitingly,
for so long.
Confusion settled in.
Who can I trust,
Lord?, And who
(should) can I let in?
I felt like a bruised
reed, and a petal,
ripped by the
aggression of someone's
   hands.

An archaic soul,
lacking the drive
to be beautiful again.
Arch shaped,
like petals bowing,
but you held my
face, and palmed
my cheeks
in your hands,
and told me to rise
above, my dust,
and beautiful
stand!

Ashes Traded for Beauty

Lily,
lilac, beautiful flowers.
Women,
you are who Christ says you are period.

A Bride (in the Eyes of Christ)

Christ thinks that you are a
porcelain doll,
breathtaking
in his eyes.
Beautifully, donned,
rainbow in his skies.
Fluttery hair,
beautiful hips.
He says that you are
splendorous,
beautiful nature,
and when He sees you,
it reminds Him of
rubies for lips.
He says,
"You are my
daughter,
your hair,
I will kiss."
Treasures.

Your heart was broken,
but now you are free
because you have found
your love in Jesus.

His Heartbeat Yearns for Her

Freckle-faced,
chocolate-skinned
dark girl.
Doe-faced
Latina princess.
Mahogany lovely
complexion.
You are simply
beautiful because
you were styled in
the palm of His
hands.

Asian beauty,
African,
chocolate-mocha
queens,
you are beautiful
because you
are treasured by
the King.

Mediterranean
butterscotch beauty,
richly blended
with a tan.
His fingers,
embroidered
your elegance,
with His rich
love.

Indian, burned
brown,
silky-haired,
Aboriginal queens,
you inspire God's
heartbeat.

Light-faced,
butter-pecan
interracial girl.

Vibrant melon
honey,
you were a
delight when He
made you, and
you are simply
brilliant because you
were styled in the
palm of His hands.

THE FRAGRANCE OF A BEAUTIFUL SOUL (LEARNING TO LOVE MYSELF)

A smooth gleaming surface
   is all that it is.
Her passion for tapestry,
   makeup,
drawn on her skin.
Her rose petal dresses fly
in the wind when she strides.
She's a beautiful sculpture
   drawn on a grid.

Her garments are beautiful,
   flow
nicely on her curves, but she
   quietly
sits, a queen like Ester,
   beauty is loud,
being heard.

Her eyes are like gold,
they call her a jewel.
Her words are like honey,
dripping, fountains of ooze.
She tells them she holds the
   likeness
of Christ's beauty.
Her body like a flask
of weeds, wrapped in
   ceramic, jewellery.

Elegant and Beautiful

When people see her, they see a bride,
beautiful elegant woman in the store.

They are awestruck by her glimmer.
Her elegant mannerisms, and good-natured
spirit are what people adore.

She is buttery, her beautiful black face
shimmers, then people say she is
sleek. Her inner confidence makes her
radiantly beautiful, when she speaks.

They can't tell why she is so elegant.
It must be her clothes. It must be her
garments, the way she puts her hair in a fold.
It must be her style, the way she struts,
it must be her pose.

But it's the presence of God, that
brings and radiates the atmosphere,
the way it streams and it flows. His
presence is gorgeous, the way it
clings to the soul.

When people see her, they
	see a bride,
beautiful elegant woman in
	the store.

They are awestruck by her
	glimmer, and
her elegant nature is what
	people adore.

Chocolate Queen

Asian beauty,
African,
chocolate-mocha
queens
who feel
beautiful on the
inside because they
are treasures in their
fathers' eyes.

Mediterranean
butterscotch beauty,
richly blended
with a tan.

Indian, burned
brown,
silky-haired
Aboriginal queens,
who've been
told they
inspire their
fathers' heartbeats.

Light-faced,
butter-pecan
interracial girl,
vibrant melancholy
honey.
You were a
delight when He
made you, and
you are simply
brilliant because
you are bedazzling
to your father.

BALLERINA-DRESS DAUGHTER

I wanted to be treasured and
made vulnerable
again, like a little girl.
I wanted Dad to see
my ballerina dress
while I danced
around to Mozart's music,
as my body would twirl.
I wanted Dad to fix my
rosy dress, to make sure that
the strings wouldn't cause
any mess.
In his arms, an escape,
my body undressed.
Six years old. It didn't
matter, those days we
were free.
He told me about the birds,
sexual chatter, and about
honey bees. He turned
away every boy with cruel
intent who hoped to
draw me in with allure.
He made sure that I was
like a porcelain doll kept
hidden in stores. Oh, Dad
was so handsome, and his
humour is what people
adored. Memories of him
dancing, playing clown
characters, and dressing
my sores. I'm a lady now;
I do womanly things on
my own. Although I'm
independent,
I'm still his ruby that glows.

TREASURE IN MY FATHER'S EYES

Dad smiles
at my
chocolate skin.
He says, I am his
beautiful
girl.

He taught me
purpose.
He says that I am
his.

He taught me
to love myself,
whether or not
you accept
it.

He taught me
to fold my legs
neatly when
I have my dress
on.

He taught me
to cling to
what is right.

He taught me
to keep my
shoulders back
and hold my
head high. He
taught me that I
deserve to strut
red carpets because
I am his queen.

My father delights
in me. He assures
me that I
am beautiful.
He assures me
that I am a
masterpiece.

Everything he
taught me
speaks volumes
because I am
Daddy's princess.

I'm a Beautiful Red Rose

I am a beautiful red rose
    sheltered beneath a glass.
God's precious image, I am a
    symbol of his craft.
Within me lies a nature of
    delicacy and eloquence.
For I am a women of quality,
    virtue, and excellence.
Within me lies uprightness
    and inner beauty.
My image is translucent;
    the world can see right
    through me.
I am a rose unfolding its
    petals to express its inner
    beauty.
My character is enlightening,
    like the radiance shown
    from a ruby.
I am a sacred Crystal glass,
    of great value and worth.
I have risen past the barriers
    of thorns, stone, and dirt.
Clear and transparent,
    without camouflage or
    mask.
I am a red rose sheltered
    under untainted glass.

Rhyming One Beautiful Queen

Your heart was
once broken
small,
cleaved like a clove.

Beauties not
in riches, garments, or
    clothes,
like a sun
I will pour
my beautiful rose.

I will water you
like a petal, unfold
to see your beauty.
You are a queen.

Your struts are
fanciful, you're
a ruby it seems.

Persona, priceless,
the beauty of queens.

Porcelain doll,
breathtaking
in my eyes.

Beautifully donned,
you're my beautiful
bride.

"Face Like the Sun": Qualities of Mine

His face looked something
 like the moon's,
reflecting, sparkling, every
 time he smiled.
His hair sparkled, and was
 like coils,
silky, but thick curls.
His build was like Morris
 Chestnut's,
eyes like daisies,
teeth perfectly aligned.
His face like the sun's, with a
 tint of brown.
He appeared Puerto Rican,
 with an African twist,
except I couldn't tell whether
 he was Spanish
or just mixed.
His height was six foot five,
and he walked like thunder
 dancing around the sky.

His ways were like lilies,
blossoming for me to see,
and his lips smooth like
 caramel,-chocolate
 liquefied.
I'm infused in his presence,
on tropical vibes
rather on a tropical island.
I think this is mine
because it is what I envisage,
fitting the category
like shapes in a puzzle.
His walk like Nas's beats,
speech like Gerald Levert's,
formed oracles as the waters
 rippling my body,
echoing in my ears, weaving
 throughout my body.

His feet the length of
  liquorice,
and his fragrance the odour
  of powder.
His tongue sweet like
  cherries,
and his breath as the winds;
cool, fresh, and mystique,
like fresh mints.
Seen his presence caressing
  the trees,
and every time he spoke,
the trees gently swayed.
When our eyes kissed,
his hands weaved its paint,
galloping to warm seasons,
beating to the beating and
  dancing.
Our eyes met, flaming with
  passion,
and when he spoke, my body
  laughed,
and when I spoke, he was
  hypnotized,
and when he sang, felt like I
  was mesmerized.
These are the qualities of
  mine.

FREEDOM

I have broken past the barricades
of the mire and the clay
and have risen above my fiery days,
for every evil and inequity has been distinguished from my life,
and ever since He has showered me with the seeds of love and has
called me His wife.
And He has purged and transformed me, and in my life He has emerged and danced before me,
and many times I have felt like the trees, swaying my leaves back and forth to the tickling of His breeze.
And when I was bickering in defeat,
I heard the voice of my Lord vividly,
and His words were like music,
soothing to my ear,
and I felt liberation, like a flower unfolding its petals without fear.
I unfold my arms and my heart
and give Him praise.
Within me, He has planted treasures, like a gardener, watching his rose inside a glass.
I am valuable like a rose inside of a vase.

He has satisfied my soul with
the blessings He brings,
and the rest of my days onto
Him, I will sing!

LIBERTY IN JESUS

We are born into destruction and shame.
Shaped in iniquity and a slave to sinful chains,
He spared my life from a tormenting maze
where the unrighteous spend their everlasting days.
I hear whispers through the darkness
echoing words of guilt.
  (There is therefore now no condemnation, Romans 8:1.)
And I feel the chains of destruction pulling me back to filth.
I hear the rattling of chains, crushing beneath my feet and hands.
I'm feeling free like an ocean dancing before the sand.
Jesus is a rekindling fire, reflecting rays of light,
His love so strong that it can pierce through the inner depths of man.
Thank God he gave me a change.
I hear your voice whispering softly saying, "I'm proud of you."
Your love is an ocean that I drown into.
The Jesus inside of me is a switch that lights up a room.
I am caught in a web of my passion for you,

but like a never-ending
   maze, I am trapped in
   you,
and like a butterfly liberating
   its wings, you broke my
   cocoon.

HOPEFUL

Liberation, oh how He tickles me.
Temptation, no need because
the spirit fills me.
He flows my soul with everlasting love,
showering me with passion from above.
I look up and now have hope—
I can cope with the pressures of life.
I am His wife and within me lies power and diligence.
Ambition, I break through the barriers of my unseen chance.
Miraculously, He already defeated my foes through His name,
so now I am free to dance.
I am accelerating past the doubts of minds.
I see, I live, far from blind.
Caressed mysteriously by the power of His love.
Looking to the Heavens, my head staying above.
I no longer feel sad.
I lift up my hands to my heavenly dad.
I don't have to smoke zest to fill voids.
I am free. All of my bondages
He destroyed.

Like the bees getting the
nectar, so He fills me
with His secrecy. I am
overwhelmed with happy
thoughts.
Thank you, Lord! For
   releasing me.

It Bothers You

Does it bother you
that I click my heels,
and my body stands tall
as a mannequin on display?
Did it bother you that I
    didn't
crush under your piercing
words when I shot up
like a rose in the day?
You should see the way you
looked at me, because my
    eyes
lit up like a model with a
    barrette.
I saw the way she frowned
when I did well in school;
she thought that I would be
chained to her words when
she called me a fool.

Like the princess that I am,
I forever shine like a jewel.
I am like a rose, well
    groomed.
Does it bother you
that success streams
through my blood?
Does it crush you that
my face gleams in the sun?
When you put me
down, I will run!
When you belittle me
like a bird,
I will still rise to the sun.

I will stand strong.
I will not allow myself to be
    overturned
by your flood.
I saw her get mad when I
    hugged myself,
with love.

Jealousy Kills

Why do you speak ill,
when my dreams are high like a bird's?
Why do you hate me
and then kill me with your words?
Instead of speaking a blessing,
you're quick to speak a curse.
When everything I say drops honey, and I walk confidently.

From afar you saw me progressing,
that's why you were drooping your brows.
You saw dollar bills in my potential,
that's why you frowned.
I am a confident woman,
wearing black on my skin.
Your words are ever ready to pierce me,
sharper than radars that trim.

Why did you neglect to speak positive things?
Was it the way that my skin gleamed like gold on a ring?
I can't help that royalty runs through my line.
It was the Christ who purchased me,
and He's what made my lineage shine.
I am a confident woman wearing
her black on her skin,
but my confidence wouldn't be possible
if I didn't have Christ as my kin.

You were afraid because
you saw success.
I know who I am.
I *am!* a beautiful queen,
and as long as I live, I will
   always stand.

I Am Sacred

Sacred, I am.
Ocean liberating itself before the sand.
Sky, I am.
Bring sunlight and water to the land.
Springs of water, I am.
Cleaning one from the filth.
Words of encouragement, I am.
Relieving your mind from the guilt.
Restitution, I am.
"A backboard one can lean on.
A pillow, I am.
One can lay their head and sleep on.
Happiness I am.
Springs forth are seeds of joy.
Fruitility, I am beautiful.
Hopefully, I'll have a baby boy.

REJECTION

I yearn to answer the call
these corridors, so I crawl,
open door—
what is beyond this wind?
So I crave them like an
    addict.
For your information my
    kind got talents; we rap
    and sing ballads,
aspirations, and gifts,
and we are more than just
    rum and spliffs
because they don't cater to
    us—here
they believe that if they give
    us a mantle we'll fail.
They believe that all we'll
    amount to is drugs and
    jail,
but black people are more
    than just cold and frail,
but our skin colour is the
    colour of sun,
but let me tell you what I
    mean when I
I thought I unlocked the
    door to his heart
with my radiant smiles
as he looked outside
the wind, embraced his limbs
as the sun pierced my eyes.
Usually the wind would
    collide,
brush my black face,
lift my moods,
taste my kinky hair,
intrude my space.
But this time butterflies,
    inside, did paint
my clouds with rainy days,
so as I witnessed signs of his
    rainy day,

tension within his cloud,
it disrupted my soul
seeing his angled eyebrows
 interrupt my soul.
You're too black.
So my heart departed from
 the sun,
made me know what was
 going on—
rejection.
I could tell because his
 thoughts were interrupted
 by ringing bells of their
words.
Rejection.
I thought I had unlocked
 his heart with my soul
 Ashanti black beauty,
but I was left with miseries,
rejection
'cause he was closed in,
 tampered, saturated with
 trickery.

I wanted the rays of my
 smile to emblazon his
 sadness,
dip him in a pool of moral
 gladness,
but rejection—
these words that he exhaled
 fractured my mind,
leaked inside my soul,
affected my incite of
black beauty
because his words were
 intrusive,
elusive,
my black beauty blurred
with words of
rejection
that left my mind in
 confusion.
I wanted to replace his
 ignorance with my black
 beauty, "intrude him, "
beauty like soot that rises to
 the air,

engrave his heart with my
    spell and take him there
to my black beauty
because I wanted to tattoo
    his lips with my black kiss,
but his thoughts were
    manipulated by ringing
    bells of their—
rejection.
I thought I unlocked the
    door to his heart with my
    black smiles
but he wouldn't let me
    divorce his mind from
    thoughts of these racist
    and
perilous times,
so rejected.
We were just friends back
    then,
thought that we could be
    more than,
but he wanted to keep our
    distance like memories of
    my playpens,
so rejected
because my skin tone kept
    us from being more than
    mates,
so rejected
that left me feeling more
    than hate
and disconnected,
so he divorced me,
rejected,
so I felt rejected when I
    walked out of my house,
thinking maybe if I preened
    my hair he would accept
    me as a spouse,
but I grew up as a black
    queen, kinky hair,
rats and mouse,
but to choose you, should I
    reject

Jamaican dialect? You done
 know at your European
 expense,
so as I thought, should I
 leave or to European
 ideals be attached
so our skins clash like a
 boxing match?
Rejection
This is what made me feel
 like I had to divorce
 myself from this bloody
picture-
rejection
because you abandoned me
 when you abandoned
 the other side of your
 mixture,
so your pleas of I'm a mixed
 breed
my mother's white and I
 have a dark skin-toned
 dad,
but you guys, he rejected me
 because he said that my
 skin colour is too black,
but you see, when he
 rejected me
he neglected everything he
 has—
Ashanti black beauty
because every time I seen
 her, and you
felt like her and my pigment
 battled in the room.
Then you had to choose
like you were confused
 about your African roots.
Face it, you neglected our
 skin tone
like dark-skin girls pushed
 to the backside of music
 videos,
like never really seeing black
 girls in herbal essence
 commercials,

like never really seeing
    coloured cartoons and
    band aids the colour of
    maroons,
so rejection.
You made me feel this way,
like our colour was a
    disgrace,
rejection.
I divorced myself from these
    lies
that society replays in our
    minds
that our skin colour is like
    lice,
because my colour is like the
    sun's lights-
black queens, not
    stereotyped black fiends,
    but black queens
with the expressions of
    queenly persona—
you guys, we are black
    queens.

Memories of My Father

I open up a chapter.
I am reading a love letter.
He wrote to me.
A book that calls me
a women of God.
A love chapter that reminds me
that I am His blooming
rose, in a field.
A love poem that
tells me that I am a
bountiful queen.

I am the bride of Christ.
He makes music to my ears.
He whispers beautiful symphonies,
and in a bottle collects all of my tears.

Like a windup doll,
preserved in a chest.
I am a beautiful windup doll,
rose patterns along my dress.

I cherish myself.
I used to look beyond.
I used to search below
because my father was gone.

I used to plaster makeup on my face,
wore an evening dress to the prom.
I made sure that I was beautiful
and that my makeup was drawn.

I made sure that I was attractive,
looking for Daddy in all kinds of sets.
I was lost, but now I am found.
I am a beautiful treasure, like Queen Ester wearing a crown.

I am awestruck by His presence.
He calls me his daughter.
He is breathtaking to the eyes—
the love of the Father.

The memories of an absentee father—
they have been restored.
He replaced them with His presence.
I am no longer unsure—
whose I am!

I am captivated by the love of the Father.

Beautiful to perception.
A diva in His eyes.
You! are His daughter.
He calls you His bride.
You are His beautiful bead, lovely in His eyes.
He thinks you are awesome because He made you
in the image of Christ.

Restored Lily

Her dress was torn.
Her cotton dress
was bleeding.
Her wounds were *so*! loud,
her heart was constantly
speaking.

Where am I?
Where can I go?
his hands tore my
insides—
ripped my beautiful soul.
Her words were loud.
Her breath was heavy.

Her mind fell into
despair.
Her heart was
empty.
She felt like a wreck.

She fell
to the floor.
Looking for her worth,
like a woman hoping that
a man would buy her a ring
in the store.
Won't someone notice
me?

Won't someone
pick the tag off
my heart?
Won't someone
notice that I'm
like a beautiful
fragrance?
Like a Mona Lisa
painting—
gold streams,
rubies?
Baroque art?

I was raped.
I was left.
My worth
is nowhere to be found.
My heartbeat is like
a clock racing.
Ticking away—
it pounds.
But, I have to wear
my crown.

I was abused.
I am lingering on.
A pole is where I make
money to make sure
the bills are paid.

I wish someone could
notice me.
I wish someone could
tell me I'm beautiful.
It's in the Bible.
He died to tell me
I will be okay.

I Feel Fat

I am fat.
I eat ice cream all day,
hoping that the hurtful
words of my stepfather
will go away.
I wear big clothes
to hide the love handles,
which peek out of me.
I am tired of my
weight.
I hope that I can hear Him
calling me—
His beautiful girl.

I am tired.
I feel disgusted.
I feel broken down,
and defeated.
I heard about the cross
and how
He died for me.

I heard that
His blood stained
the cross to
tell me of my worth.
I was told that
I am deserving
of His forgiveness.

I don't need to
beat myself down
in my room.
He showed me my
worth.

The Media Told Me Who I Am

I can't run away.
I am bombarded with images
of how women should look.
The media says I have
to be cool to get
a boyfriend.
I am constantly fixated
on dating,
teen drinking,
and going out with friends.

Can somebody understand
I am just a teen?
Low confidence.
I hope I can
see myself,
beautiful again.

I can't get away—
the Father keeps calling me
and telling me to pray.

If I keep watching television
one day longer,
I may be pressured to
to give my body away.

The story of grace:
Christ said I'm strong.
The words in my
head, they just won't
go away.
All I need to
do is go down on my knees
and pray.

Crystal Rose

Valuable

Lipstick,
music,
fashion,
Jezebel,
abusing drugs,
to feel good about
my heart.
He died thinking
I was a princess.

BLOOD-ROYAL OF HEAVEN

Blood-royal of Heaven.
Jesus Christ died, and shed
   crimson blood on the cross,
   it was reddened.
To profess His love for us.
To make a plea like merchants
   in a slave market.
Buying slaves, a profession
of his love.
You were worth dying for.
Blood-royal of Heaven when
   He died on the cross,
He bargained for your soul,
like pirates on a ship
   searching for gold.

WE ARE ROYALTY IN HIS EYES

I am *constantly*
trafficked by men,
abused, belittled.
I have never heard the
message of Christ,
my heart hurting.

I heard Christ
would love me,
take my pain away.
I heard that Christ
died to tell me that
I am valuable.
I read that He thinks
that I am delightful,
and stunning—I read that
  He thinks that I am
  attractive,
like barrettes in a braid.
I have never met Christ.

I heard He's a man
who came down to
save me from
the brutality of an
abuser's hands.

I lost my worth
that night,
when he came in to
rape me.

She lost her worth,
when she gave her
body away.

She always asks,
"Where does my
worth lie?"
Who does Christ say I am?
He died a brutal
death.

He was crucified
to save me.
I'm His Tinker Bell,
and He's my Peter Pan.

No More

No more scars.
He washed them away.
I read His love letter
and how He died
to tell me I will be okay.

My pain—
my promiscuity
after the rape.
After the continual
readings of the night
rewound in my mind
like tape.

He took all my sins.
He took all my scars.
He let me know
I was worth it
when He died for
my heart.

I don't need to carry
low self-esteem.
I don't need to
embrace the painful
memories.
He took them to the cross
when He was beaten.
He took the shame to the
   cross.
He took everything!

I am a Taiwanese girl.
I want to be happy.
He made love
to my heart,
and He gave me significance.

I Don't Need to Search Any Longer

In His words
I found
significance.
He gave me worth.
I don't need to
sleep around to
feel good about myself.

Christ died for my
soul because
He thinks that I am
valuable.
He died
to restore my
soul and He makes
me feel significant.

He makes me feel
beautiful,
cherished,
intelligent, and literate.

I don't need to listen
to the words that
people have spoken
over my life—
I refuse to
listen to negativity.

I've found significance.
I've found joy!
I have found who
I am ever since
I've encountered
Jesus Christ's love.

Confidence

I am old.
I am single.
I'm now a confident girl.
In my heart
I carry Christ's words.
In my soul,
there is a *sweet*
presence clinging
to me.
I bask in the most
precious glory
when I am in Jesus!

I ignore their
words.
I pay no
attention to their
laughter.

I flip the pages
of my life
moving forward
in chapters.
I am single.
I can be confident
in myself.
I can
hold my head up
because someone
beyond the sky
loves me.
God cherishes me!

Her Worth Redeemed

You are beautiful wives,
yet the media is distorting
   His crucifix, why?
To let us know our worth.
He was bruised in His side.
He purchased us
with His blood.
For us He flew to the sky.
He wanted to let us know
He's the groom, and
she's His beautiful bride.

Her Seditions

Her seditions, why don't men divorce her?
Her yellow charms are deluding, and her ways suffocate many.
Her ploys, yet men cannot abort her.
Her pigments eluding, yet they fall prey to her spell.
She possesses pink gums and sparkling brown eyes,
reflecting pupils of a dime, but I possess a bird's-eye view.
The wisdom of a soothsayer, Plutocratic, filling your mental attenuation.
An ambrosia of words transcended from oracles of the divine.
I satiate with amorous pursuits of the mind.
Yet, men lay pliable to her seditions, as she craftily captures their hearts—
paintings of touches as thistles of art.
Stroking, but unable to restore streams onto Sahara.
Plucking her plectrum, yet she lays obsolete.
Her plight is predictable, and her inner, decked with jaundice.
She tawdrily expresses lingual of love, yet nostrils burn for her redolence,
as the nature's desolation without moonbeams.

She is an artificial saga so,
adorned with berry-like
vessels, yet multiples
cannot unveil her guise.
She is as a still life, surfaced
without spectrum, yet
men cannot unravel her
myth.
Her plethora of karmas
tarmac many, but a
queen's ways are eternally
honourable.

Christ's Asian Princess

He's so mad that His
Angels are wrecked.
They sold His princess
for pesos and cheques.
In backyards women
ferociously raped on their
  steps.
He loves because He wants
  to
let us know we are not
belugas, chicken heads, or a
swine in a sty.
The very same God that they
put in a tomb and confined
is the same God who
  purchased us
with His blood like a
  merchant
searching for dimes.
He calls me His princess and
  says
He's not after my fashion
  and clothes.
His passion unfolds.
He merely wants my heart
to stop bleeding, as
his passion unfolds.
We don't need to look for
  love—
He cherishes us like a castle
  in Rome.
He stopped my hurt sister,
when I found out that
His grace covers me.
No matter what we've
done in the past, we can
  stand
tall like beautiful glass.
We can shine and dazzle like
  stones
because our worth surpasses
  rubies, and gold.

Beautiful Mannequin in a Glass to Him

When you walk
you should do it
with confidence!
Like a dad who is
proud of his daughter.

I know He thinks I am
wonderful.
I stand like a porcelain doll
   in a glass.

I stand tall like Queen
Ester.
I am a woman of class.
I put value on myself
because my worth
is found in His blood.

I refuse to let pain fester.
I refuse to hold on to it!
He died to take all of my
   shame.

Move forward.
Give him your doubts!

I am no carbon copy—
I am a porcelain dolly.
I am beautiful, and
glamorous.
I *am* a treasure in my
father's eyes.
I am God's queen.

ROYAL HIGHNESS

I look in the mirror
to see my black skin colour.
I am proud.
Look how it suits me.

He soothes me.
He's enamoured
by my beauty.

I heard that He is so
in love, that His eyes
shine like moonbeams.

My body's like earth art.
I work hard to polish me.
My inner beauty shines
   forth,
and my spirit is precious,
like pottery.

You are a beautiful lady;
my sister,
my friend,
together
let's see our worth as
   commodity.

Let's be enamoured with
the women who
looks back in the mirror.
Let's celebrate
being His clay—
so that He can
exercise His sovereignty.

Black and Beautiful

So beautiful,
my beautiful gold
   complexion.
Eyes like a ruby lens—
beautifully
looking through me,
in reflections,
in dimensions.
Mine is like a jubilee.
It's soothing me.
My essence is
like jewellery.
My kink is grooming me.

My confession—
my kinks,
my protection.
Even when
slaves used it in
winter depressions,
the cotton on my head
is rejected.
It is blended with
weave extensions,
looking like strangled
seaweeds embedded.
My transmitted
follicles are infected,
lacking mineral dressings,
after pressing.

Afrocentric Beauty

Afrocentric natural's
　neglected.
It is in executive sessions—
now it's in the traumatic
section.
Eurocentric satin is accepted,
but Eurocentric platinum
is expensive.
Kinky is seen as offensive.
Deception in offices
made her feel like a
　cockatrice.
Rejection on documents—
her locks and twists.
Conception like a fallen mist.
She now cut it off,
and her directions
　anonymous.
She tossed her pick,
and missed the symbol
of a drawn-in fist,
and that being black is
　strong.
It hurt like a throbbing cyst,
to follow trends.

MARVELLOUS AFRO

Let's bring it back to the seventies,
when Afros weren't removable,
when Afros were so beautiful to the soul.
My goal is to realize the beauty of my whole.
Extolled from an Afro chic,
the beauty of the hold.
You remind me of mutton merino—
soft brand, like African sheep.

HE GOT MARRIED TO ME ON THE CROSS

She is black and beautiful.
Slim, Coca Cola bottle.
He looks back, and
He heals her heart.
He tells her she is beautiful.
In His eyes, she is
a bedazzling jewel.
She is a princess
a beam in His eyes.
She is breathtaking
to Him because she is His wife.

Continue to Rise

I will continue to rise beyond the dirt.
I am clay being caressed inside the potter's hands.
I am the day bringing sunlight to the land.
I am the rain showering the flowers, and the trees.
The birds. I bring worms to their beaks.
The leaves, how they have freedom in the presence of the wind.
I win and I break, I pick myself up again.
Powerful, virtuous, excellent, I am.
I strive for perfection, in the way God created the land.
I am amazed at how everything is so proportioned.

River of Rain

Life's a struggle when you think everyone's your enemy.
Sometimes I feel locked behind bars, like I've done a felony.
I feel lost and motionless like a beat without its melody.
Please, God, rescue me.
I'm held captive to your own deep hurts and pain.
Drained and dry like the Sahara Desert without rain.
Decaying like a star whose lost her fame.
Sorrows, loneliness, and despair are drowned into alcohol bottles.
The remains of painful memories have hardened me into stone, like bone fossils.
I exhale the remains of deep scars from my body and my mind.
Watching it escape with the fumes in the sky,
because the only thing that soothes me are the tears I cry.

Discrimination during University Years

It's 2005.
Throughout my daily life,
 I am confronted with
 borders.
Challenges, obstacles,
 barriers, and horrors.
Illusions, seclusions, my life
 is like the Great Wall.
Boxed in cocoons, hurdles,
 and igloos.
My fear is borders,
 circumstances, my life
 concealed.
Closed, separation, linear, my
 family photo is revealed.

Racial Borders

I see borders of
   discrimination dividing
   minorities from the upper
   class.
And I see racism in today's
   society, repeated from the
   past.
I am tired of the media
   portraying unexplained
   images among blacks.
So I dream about what it
   would be like to live in a
   world of true liberation,
since minorities are suffering
   from the effects of veiled
   racism,
and I see dominant classes
   gaining undeserved
   privileges,
while society is being
   affected by racial images.
Minority groups are
   constantly portrayed as
   savages,
and I can't seem to find
   plenty of black dolls,
   or maroon coloured
   bandages.
I can't walk down the streets
   without being resented.
And I don't see minorities
   in newspapers widely
   represented.
I am determined to break
   through the barriers of
   racial borders
that have caused internal
   scars, distress, and many
   horrors.

The borders of racism have risen like China's Great Wall,
but with inner strength and hope, racial borders shall fall.

Beautiful Gaze

I gaze out of my window towards Heaven, and I visualize what life would be like behind the clouds.

I am intrigued by his creation of nature, humans, and my own eyebrows.

I close my eyes and painted in my mind is a highway of jewellery in Heaven, and when the rays of light from the sun cover the earth, I feel the warmth of His presence.

He walks on his bridge towards my window at night, and His presence is soothing to me.

I look beyond my window, seeing nature blossoming, reminding me of His beauty.

His robe is printed with white pearls, and His crown patterned neatly with rubies.

I look out my window to Heaven, and he has enriched my life, so much that I feel His hug.

I see Him clothing His children when they are in need of love.

Every morning I kick my sheets off to see the birds singing in the trees.

When my window is open, I am embraced by the breeze.

I feel free like a bird outside
of my window flying in
the sky.
I look out my window to
Heaven, and I feel him
passionately decorating
me with His eyes.

Accept Christ and He Will Give You Eternal Life

She basks in his wind.
She hears his voice,
but cruelty has tarnished her
at the expense of his ploys.
She can't hear anymore
because of TV's noise.
Jezebel took her body,
and she became his toy.
She fiddles with her guitar.
He tells his boys
that he caught his princess,
that she became his toy.
Her breasts his playground.
Her soul is blackened,
   destroyed.
Her body stinks.
It reeks of his loins.
Intruder,
she lays unmoving,
waiting for God to fill all her
   voids.
No direction, he says receive
   it with joy.
So much brokenness,
from Taiwan to the streets of
   Detroit.
She fiddles with her guitar.
He tells his boys
that he caught his princess,
that she became his toy.

My Story

Beautiful,
like a statue on the horizon,
her body was like a flask of
   weeds.
She stood tall,
flawless,
like the wind blowing
   through the trees.
Confident nature,
poised—
elegant queens.
Her brother raped her,
stripped her clothes,
jewellery and sleeves.
Now she hides behind rags
as if she were plagued with
   disease.
Behind veils, eyes peering
   out to see.
Can someone please save
   her?

The Son set us free.
Get out of those clothes,
   Tamar,
You are a beautiful queen!

What Does It Mean?

What does it mean to be the potter's clay?
It means to be easily moulded and well-shaped.
It means to be free from dirt, filth, or stain.

THE ESSENCE OF LIFE (PERSONAL TESTIMONY)

Some people are shielded
from the true beauty of
the world.
Some from happiness, some
from love, and some
haven't seen the true
beauty of a pearl.
Some have been hurt and
others have been cursed,
and some have been masking
their unhappiness by
wearing sexy skirts.
Some have been drowning
their unhappiness in
liquor,
and others have been
stripping for their comfort
to get richer.

Well, I examined my life to
see my error,
and I realized I'd been
bound to many guilty
terrors.
Bruised as a child from
loneliness and shame,
so I became a slave to
worries and pain.
Feeling like a stranger
among my friends,
so only freedom was my pad
and a pen.
My paper was an outlet,
where I could release my
fears and my cries,
because the only companion
I had were my tears and
my eyes.

Some people find comfort
   from the finer things in
   life.
Some from external beauty,
   and some find it in
   husbands, and some in
   their wife.

As for me, the only thing
   that I am missing is
   spiritual intimacy with
   Christ.

You Are a Champ

You can stand.
White horses galloping one day.
One day your king will be riding your way.

Ex-Boyfriend: Courtship

I won't break it, Sugar; you can trust me with your heart.

I won't break it. Love is about spirituality and inner beauty, not about getting naked. Even though intimacy defines the true essence of love.

True intimacy is void without getting to know the true presence above.

I have never been a venomous snake hiding beneath the grass, or a crafty Karma, hiding beneath a mask. I am me, a beautiful red rose shielded within a glass. Reflecting rays of light piercing through the inner depths of man.

I am not yet perfect, for I am being moulded in the potter's hand—so I feel free like an ocean dancing before your sand.

Or I can be your crystal, and you can be my gem, or I can be the petals of red roses upholding your stem.

Or I can simply be the wind embracing your leaves, or I can be your remedy, like Chinese tea leaves.

Or you can simply rest on me like a pillow filled with feathers, and we can get lost in the moment and make music together.

Or I can lure you into the depths of the forest from my sweet scent of roses and the aroma of apple trees, and you can get lost in the presence of my voice calling you through the breeze.

Remember, you are a majestic king and your craft is your throne.

Your crown defines your manliness, your integrity, and your home.

My words are like medicine bringing healing to your soul, and I am a summer's breeze releasing your life from the cold.

Your dreams may have foreshadowed a rude awakening and your hopes of finding true love may even have faded, but remember, you're kingly, you're princely, like holy ground you are sacred.

Boo, you can trust me with your heart, since I won't break it.

Why He Loves Me

Why he loves me, it
    surpasses the whole,
captivates me as it captures
    my soul.
Don't need a man to say
    your assets are gold.
Don't need make to feel
    your stature is gold.
Ya more beautiful than the
    palace in Rome,
Yeah.
The fact of the guise
some put makeup to capture
    his eyes.

Caught in a snare, like
foxes and deer.
Cupid came round, shocked
    by his pierce,
crazy in love,
got lost in his glare
when we locked in a stare.

Beautiful

My beautiful gold complexion. Eyes like a ruby lens. Beautifully looking through me, in reflections of dimensions. My makes like jubilees, it's soothing me my essence, like jewellery. My kinks finally grooming me. My confession. My kinks my protection, even when slaves used it during winter depressions. But the cotton on my head's rejected; it's blended with weave extensions, looking like strangled seaweed embedded. My sexually transmitted follicles are infected by salon orgies, in professions. Burnt with hot comb foreplays. Smelling like solar arrays in salon domains, strands feeling like burnt Du Maurier.

Afro-centric natural's neglected in executive sessions—now it's in the traumatic section. As Eurocentric satin is accepted, but damn Eurocentric platinum fabric is expensive, and paying taxes for synthetic investments because laws have been implemented in Baltimore, in colleges, and professions, implementing weaves as incentives as kinky is seen as offensive, causing awkwardness. Deceptions in offices trying to keep her kinky anonymous, and now she's off the list on resumés and documents feeling incompetent because of her locks and twists, now seeking an optometrist, shielding it with toxins, trying to shield it with iodine and toxins.

My celibate, now like fried halibut, limp, fallen. and anorexic. I can't help it didn't get up when I pressed it.

Kinky's in depression and barely seen in Hollywood daringly, unless it looks like straight and wavy of Halle Berry's, but rarely I love me without cherishing a hair piece, or thinking hair weaves in mental dictionaries.

So, I kept the weave till it looked like it was charity, unbearably, until my weave itched terribly, needing Dr. Miracle for therapy she kept her natural to look beautiful for clarity. Let's bring it back to the seventies, when Afros weren't removable, and bring our cuticles back to the toes. When Afros were so beautiful to the soul. My goal is to realize the beauty of my whole, extolled. From an Afro-Chic, the beauty of the hold you remind me of mutton merino soft brand, like African sheep fold soft cotton strands worth the colour of a deep gold, like a chocolate candy. Your hair feels like cotton candy to my teeth, hold far from a cheap toll the sight like tiny rippling seashores. We kiss, feeling the richness, your enrichment feeling like briskness, the colour of Twix Sticks of our descendants reason my skin like apple-cinnamon, it was dipped in Africa's jurisdiction, colour

cropped like Egyptians. Did
I mention hair thick like
gold, dimensions like golden
pendants, its presence like
gold investments of a 25
carat gold fluorescence,
rich circumference? Doesn't
feel like 100 percentage
of a weaved-in synthetic
in Texas when we French
kiss, and caress in a cotton
maze-beauty penetrates
through cropped affections,
like collections of livestock
productions. That's why I'm
loving cotton pleasures it
feels like I'm cuddling cotton
sweaters.

1 Exhaled the Remains

I exhaled the remains of
 deep sores from my mind,
watching it escape, fuming
 from the emptiness inside,
wishing that I too can escape
 with the fumes in the sky
'cause the only beauty
 reflected were the tears I
 would cry,
drowning into liquor bottles.
Joy and laughter hardening
 into bone fossils,
my life was veiled from the
 exhales of smoke through
 my nostrils.
For fear and shame reflected
 nothing but years of
 pain tears engraved in
 my facial expressions,
 reflecting nothing but
 depression.
I mean, gazing at my
 image I felt so defined,
 and restricted, by how
 the world saw me as
 beautiful, so I felt so
 demised
'cause I was lost without
 motion, like the day
 without it's ocean.

They acted like pussy-cat
 dolls was the standard of
 true beauty, when truly
 they took tainted. God's
 beauty, and stole it,
Consumed with fumes and
 then being trashed.
I felt like Jews being gassed,
so I gasped because behind
 masks. I would hide. I felt
 like I was stifling God's
 beauty behind a guise of
 distorted beauty.

Part Two

In God's eyes, she was beautiful. He made Eve beautiful, so gorgeous, like daffodils or the unfolding of a blooming rose, in the cool of the day. Satan's, like I'll mess with her family, -was so jealous of Eve's beauty. I guess he was angry 'cause God kicked him out of his throne for allowing pride to get in his way, for allowing evil to manipulate his mind. God says I won't let him escape, but God told Eve she was beautiful, but yet she didn't believe, and God told her don't eat the apple right there, Eve, in the midst of the trees, but Satan told her if she ate the apple she would be God, like the myths of the Greeks, so the prince of deceit told her a lie, insist she believe. Imagine how God felt when he found Adam and Eve in figments of leaves.

This is what happens in today's society. We cover up with make-up, hair styles, but wounds and shames inside of me, they stay. We cover up our greys 'cause we hate our makes entirely. When God made us intricately beautiful, can't you see? Makes like diamond rings, so beautiful, everything about your creation, body like chocolate bars on top of mars when

we're gazing. It's like seeing
stars when we're stationed
above, like tasting a plum. I
succumb to your love when
I was making your sum, so I
can't let the days slip-vanish
like vapours till I say, "Lord,
you're the man I could stay
with," passions abrasive,
lavished and placid, heart
was torn but he patched
it like drape stitch, gave
me some anklets like Vasti
bracelets, says that I'm
sacred, like Vasti in braceless,
so beautiful, everything
about your creation, for you
created my inmost being.
You knit me together in
my mother's womb (Psalms
139:13-14). I praise you
because I am *fearfully and
wonderfully made*; your
works are.

First Love

She exhaled remains of deep sores from her mind,
watching it escape, fuming form the emptiness inside,
wishing that she too can escape with the fumes in the sky
because the only friends were the tears she would cry,
drowning into liquor bottles,
joy and laughter hardening into fossils,
her life veiled from the exhale of smoke through her nostrils,
for she longed that the abuse would fade away
like a lost soul soothed by juice and Gatorade.

The truth is, she puffed the pain away
because she wanted reality to move and stay away.
She was lost without motion like the day without its ocean.
Wanting my embrace to feel like body lotion,
my self-worth decayed like a birth right renamed,
for I could not regain strength,
so I felt drained in length.

Every time I turned to smoke, liquor, and wine,
I could only find my wounds intensify.

So this is why Christ was
crucified-
that he may give life and
heal my wounds inside.
I knew I could trust God
with my heart.
He wouldn't break it.
I knew love was about
spirituality,
not about getting naked,
even though intimacy
defines the true essence
of love.
True intimacy is void without
getting to know his true
presence above.
I knew the truth because
my mom gave me Godly
advice,
introducing me to the
romance of Christ.
So I was tired of this dull
life, so I longed to gain
spiritual sight.

So- I dreamed of the palm
trees skipping to the
rhythm of the breeze,
singing as the palm trees
skip.
I remembered when honey
flowed from my lips,
and when I used to move my
hips to gospel music,
and I remembered his warm
embrace
when I was worn and faint.
He enlightened my days like
golden paint,
and when I was so weak.
So sweet was this feeling
that made my soul leap.
But life just seemed so hard
because I was heavy laden
with emotional scars.

The charm of my prince left
me marred and captive
behind bars,
but God has always been a
gleam to my dark.
He must be bringing me
through the streams like
Noah's ark,
consumed with fumes and
then being trashed.
I felt like cluttered Jews
being gassed,
so I gasped
because behind masks I
would hide.
Short skirts and fake smiles
were my disguise,
but from the mirror I could
ever hide
because they said I was a
young girl of light,
worth more than money and
pearls.

They said I was beautiful
with black curls.
Gazing at my image I felt so
revived.
Sighed because my image
symbolized
a fruit pure, holy, and ripe.
Lord, please hold me, I cried,
for fear and shame reflected
nothing but years of pain.
Tears engraved in my facial
expressions reflecting
nothing but depression,
but God wanted to sooth
her, take her mind, and
elude her
to a paradise of holy wine
and coolers,
for in his eyes she was
nothing but a ruler.

Determined, she threw off
her masks,
feeling the power of God rise
inside like filling glass,
As God laughed and blew
a breath of life into her
lungs,
reviving her heart beat like
musical drums.
So I sang to the rhythms of
his magical tunes
soothingly seeping inside like
fragrant perfumes,
like a decorated ice cream I
became his coat,
but not like alcohol with
rum and coke,
but along my corridors, I
wore garments of rubies.
I was a queen of paradise,
I wore garments and
jewellery,
I whispered to the Lord,
"Please heal the wounds and
sooth me,"
for I am just a battered
women treated cruelly."
She heard a voice whisper
back, "true beauty lies
within.
You don't have to smoke,
drink, or binge.
You are a child of God, so
lift up your chin."
I felt a faint touch,
similar to the stroking of a
paint brush.
His presence was so
strong that His essence
prolonged
as he whispered I am so fond
of being your cornerstone
to uphold you when my
corner's gone.

All the times that you have cried,
I have been there by your side drying your eyes.
You don't have to eat feces with the pigs and the swine.
As my mind unravels and unwinds,
I heard a voice calling, "My child, my child my child,"
come home."

FORGIVENESS

My stepfather,
Oh you're getting old.
His goal was to get me out
of the house—get rid.
His tactic was you are
getting old,
you should have kids.
Look at me. When I was your
  age,
I left from Jamaica,
already getting paid.
Caught between two worlds.
Lord, you say be still.
All these negative words, I
  have sound mind.
Jealousy kills,
but yet he keeps saying
  you're mentally ill.
These words, they're hurting.
Quarrelling and no peace in
  the house.
Peace be still,
all of these cursings—
I am much more valuable
and beautiful, beautiful
  deserving.
I am getting older,
Everyone saying move out.
So tormenting,
him because he verbally
  abused
his daughter.
I need to forgive my
  stepfather
one day, Dad threatens.
Sometimes I am walking,
memories of yes releasing
  water.
God says to forgive my
  enemies,
I am in my early thirties now.

My house feels like juvenile
   jail, Felonies.
Forgive your enemies seventy
   times seventy.
Clear your heart from
   unforgiveness,
my daughters, kings, and
   princes,
internally, I cry,
but I didn't deserve
   forgiveness,
yet Jesus died.
So who am I not to forgive?
He comes to church,
and a war within,
I offer him a ride.

Dear Lord Jesus, I know that I am a sinner, and I ask Your forgiveness. I believe You died for my sins and rose from the dead. I turn from my sins and invite You to come into my heart and life. I want to trust and follow You as my Lord and Saviour.

Printed in the USA
CPSIA information can be obtained
at www.ICGtesting.com
LVHW020015021224
798042LV00002B/239